Let's Celebrate

LABOR DAY

BY Barbara deRubertis

The Kane Press
New York

For activities and resources for this book and
others in the HOLIDAYS & HEROES series, visit:
www.kanepress.com/holidays-and-heroes

Text copyright © 2015 by Barbara deRubertis
Photographs/images copyrights: Cover: © iurii/Shutterstock.com; page 1: © Rawpixel Ltd/iStock; page 3: © theboone/iStock; page 4 top: © Andreas G. Karelias/Shutterstock.com; page 4 bottom: © OliverSved/Shutterstock.com; page 5: Library of Congress, Prints & Photographs Division, LC-DIG-det-4a16452; page 6: © Everett Historical/Shutterstock.com; page 7 top: Library of Congress, Prints & Photographs Division, LC-DIG-nclc-01357; page 7 bottom: Library of Congress, Prints & Photographs Division, LC-DIG-nclc-01151; page 8 top: Library of Congress, Prints & Photographs Division, LC-USZ62-49517; page 8 bottom: Library of Congress, Prints & Photographs Division, LC-DIG-ggbain-02144; page 9: Library of Congress, Prints & Photographs Division, LC-DIG-hec-22722; page 10 top left & top right: © Monkey Business Images/Shutterstock.com; page 10 bottom left: © Dmitry Kalinovsky/Shutterstock.com; page 10 bottom right: © SpeedKingz/Shutterstock.com; page 11 top: © Nic Neufeld/Shutterstock.com; page 11 bottom: © lev radin/Shutterstock.com; pages 12 & 13: © Jim West/Alamy; page 14: © j.woottisak/Shutterstock.com; page 15: © Atomazul/Shutterstock.com; page 16: Library of Congress, Prints & Photographs Division, LC-USZ62-122076; page 17: © Jeff Greenberg/age fotostock/Superstock; page 18: © Everett Historical/Shutterstock.com; page 19: Library of Congress, Prints & Photographs Division, LC-DIG-fsac-1a35371; page 20 top: Library of Congress, Prints & Photographs Division, LC-DIG-fsac-1a34951; page 20 bottom: © Everett Historical/Shutterstock.com; page 21 top: © PhotoSky/Shutterstock.com; page 21 bottom: © bikeriderlondon/Shutterstock.com; page 22 left: Library of Congress, Prints & Photographs Division, LC-USZ62-93293; page 22 right: © Boris15/Shutterstock.com; page 23: Library of Congress, Prints & Photographs Division, LC-DIG-ppmsca-08442; page 24 top: © Sean Liew/Shutterstock.com; page 24 bottom: © a katz/Shutterstock.com; page 25 top: © Susan Chiang/iStock; page 25 bottom: © Deborah Kolb/Shutterstock.com; page 26 top: © Tyler Olson/Shutterstock.com; page 26 bottom: © bikeriderlondon/Shutterstock.com; page 27 top: © GWImages/Shutterstock.com; page 27 bottom: © bikeriderlondon/Shutterstock.com; page 28: © CA Eccles/Shutterstock.com; page 29 top: © Leonard Zhukovsky/Shutterstock.com; page 29 bottom: © Sue Stokes/Shutterstock.com; page 30 top left: © wavebreakmedia/Shutterstock.com; page 30 top right: © stockstudioX/iStock; page 30 bottom: © bikeriderlondon/Shutterstock.com; page 31 top: © michaeljung/Shutterstock.com; page 31 middle: © Monkey Business Images/Shutterstock.com; page 31 bottom: © stockyimages/Shutterstock.com; page 32: © Darrin Henry/Shutterstock.com
All due diligence has been conducted in identifying copyright holders and obtaining permissions.

Library of Congress Cataloging-in-Publication Data

deRubertis, Barbara.
  Let's celebrate Labor Day / by Barbara deRubertis.
    pages cm — (Holidays & heroes.)
  Audience: Ages 6-10.
  ISBN 978-1-57565-815-5 (library reinforced binding : alk. paper) — ISBN 978-1-57565-816-2 (pbk. : alk. paper)
  1. Labor Day—Juvenile literature. I. Title.
  HD7791.D42 2015
  394.264—dc23
                                    2015012886
eISBN: 978-1-57565-817-9

1 2 3 4 5 6 7 8 9 10

First published in the United States of America in 2015 by Kane Press, Inc. Printed in the USA.
Book Design: Edward Miller. Photograph/Image Research: Poyee Oster.

Visit us online at **www.kanepress.com**.

 Like us on Facebook
facebook.com/kanepress

 Follow us on Twitter
@KanePress

Just about the time school begins in the fall, we celebrate a national holiday called Labor Day. This holiday always falls on the first Monday of September, giving us a three-day weekend.

Labor Day honors all those who "labor"—or do skilled work—to earn wages. We celebrate the important contributions that skilled workers make to the strength and success of our country.

Because of the efforts of American workers over the years, we are one of the most productive countries in the world. And we have some of the best working conditions— such as fair pay, fair hours, and safe work places.

But working conditions were not always as good as they are today. And there is still room for improvement.

The first Labor Day was in 1882. Two groups, the Central Labor Union and the Knights of Labor, wanted to create a holiday to honor workers and give them a day off. They also wanted to call attention to the need for better working conditions.

A parade was held in New York City, and thousands of people attended.

In 1894, Congress passed an act making Labor Day a federal holiday.

A Labor Day parade in Buffalo, NY, in 1900

When did labor "unions" form—and why?

During the last half of the 1800s, many factories were built—creating many new jobs. This was called the "Industrial Revolution" because the factories' new machines made producing goods faster and cheaper.

But the working conditions in the factories were terrible. People worked 14 to 16 hours a day, six days a week. Men earned about 10 cents an hour, and women earned half as much.

Boys and girls working in the spinning room of a cotton mill

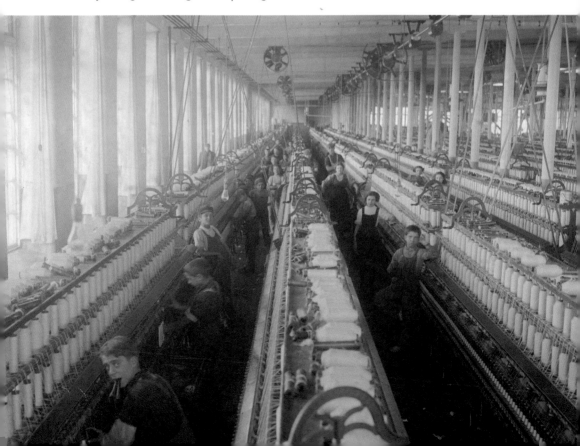

A girl at work in a textile mill

Even children worked—and they were paid less than adults. "Child labor" kept children from attending school and often ruined their health.

So workers began joining together in groups called unions. They felt they would be stronger acting together than if they tried to solve these problems alone.

Boys working in a glass factory at midnight

Workers in different trades, such as carpentry or bricklaying, formed separate unions. Some of these unions then joined together to form larger, more powerful unions.

The main goals of the unions were better wages, more reasonable hours, and safer working conditions. And they did not want children working in dangerous factories.

A Women's Trade Union League float at a Labor Day parade in New York in 1908

Educational reformers were also working to protect children. But it wasn't until 1938 that an act was passed by Congress forbidding children under 16 from working in factories and mines.

This act also set the minimum wage, or lowest amount of money a worker could be paid for an hour's work. And, for the first time, it set the maximum number of working hours in a worker's week.

Katharine Lenroot, Chief of the United States Children's Bureau, argues against child labor in 1937.

What kinds of workers can join unions?

The following workers—and many more—have unions: government workers, police, teachers, actors, airline pilots, musicians, postal workers, firefighters, ironworkers, bricklayers, electrical workers, football league players, nurses, taxi drivers, plumbers and pipefitters, utility workers, and writers.

The American Federation of Labor and Congress of Industrial Organizations (AFL-CIO) is the largest "umbrella" union in the United States. It has more than 50 member unions that represent over 12 million workers.

Members of the Communication Workers of America union, part of the AFL-CIO, march in a Puerto Rican Day parade in New York.

How do unions help workers?

When it's time for new job contracts, employer and union representatives often sit down at a table to share their ideas. This is known as "collective bargaining." If they cannot agree on everything, they "bargain" or work out a compromise.

The United Auto Workers begin contract negotiations with Ford Motor Company.

A union member casts his vote in a ballot box.

Then the union representatives present the new contract to the union members. They vote whether to accept or reject it. If they accept it, everyone signs a new contract describing his or her job and its hours, pay, and benefits.

But what happens if workers vote to reject the contract?

Sometimes union and employer representatives go back to the bargaining table again and again. Eventually, if the union members still aren't satisfied, they may take more drastic actions. Sometimes they stage a "slow-down" or a "strike." A slow-down means what it sounds like—the union members protest by working at a much slower pace.

During a slow-down, shipping containers can pile up.

Teachers on strike for better schools

But if they strike, the union members stop working. They may carry protest signs and march in picket lines outside the company.

Sometimes an employer will "break the strike" by hiring new workers to replace the union members.

And sometimes employers and workers finally reach an agreement, and everyone goes back to work.

When was the Department of Labor created?

Labor leaders worked for many years to persuade Congress to create a Department of Labor and a Secretary of Labor. The Secretary would be an important advisor to the President on labor issues. This finally came to pass in 1913.

President Woodrow Wilson made William B. Wilson (bottom right) the first Secretary of Labor in 1913.

The chief purpose of the Department of Labor is to protect workers. It helps them get fair wages and hours, retirement plans, health insurance, and safe working conditions. The department also provides training to help workers find jobs. And it gives extra help to veterans looking for jobs.

Exhibitor from the Occupational Safety and Health Administration of the Department of Labor at a South Florida Safety Expo

Who was Rosie the Riveter?

A big change happened in the labor work force after America entered the Second World War in 1941. Many of the men working in factories left their jobs to go fight in the war. But the factory jobs—and many other jobs— were an important part of the war effort, too. So the government began asking women to fill these jobs.

A poster titled "We Can Do It!" instantly became popular in 1942.

And in 1943, a song called "Rosie the Riveter" was released. It celebrated all the "Rosies" joining the labor force—and it became wildly popular.

A real-life "Rosie the Riveter" working on an A-31 Vengeance dive bomber aircraft in 1943

"All the day long,
Whether rain or shine,
She's a part of the assembly line.
She's making history,
Working for victory,
Rosie the Riveter."
—Redd Evans and John Jacob Loeb

Women answered the call for help. The number of working American women increased from 12 million to 20 million between 1940 and 1944.

A machinery operator working on parts for transport planes in 1942

A defense worker riveting as part of her training to become a mechanic at a Naval Air Base in 1942

After the war ended, some women left their jobs and returned to being homemakers. But many remained in the work force.

From that time on, women have been a large part of the American labor force.

Who was George Meany?

George Meany was a hard-working leader of the American labor movement. He believed in always doing the right thing—and had no tolerance for dishonesty.

Meany had begun his working life as a plumber. After working with several labor groups through the years, he was elected president of the American Federation of Labor—the AFL—in 1952.

A postage stamp honoring George Meany in 1994

President Gerald Ford meeting with George Meany in the White House

The other large "umbrella" union at that time was the Congress of Industrial Organizations—the CIO. In 1955, the two groups merged, and Meany was elected the first president of the combined AFL-CIO. He served as its president for 24 years.

George Meany supported other causes besides the protection of labor's interests— including the rights of women and minorities. And he supported programs like health care for retired workers.

What are some of the ways we celebrate Labor Day?

Parades march through many towns and cities. People attend festivals and fireworks displays. And speeches honoring American workers are given.

Sporting events are held—including football games, auto races, and tennis tournaments.

Families gather for picnics, cookouts, camping trips, and weekend getaways. And many people go swimming before pools and beaches close for the winter.

Labor Day is the "last hurrah" of summer!

Do some workers have to work on Labor Day, the "holiday for workers"?

Yes! Many workers spend the holiday working. Some stores offer special sales—which means store employees (a large part of the labor force) have to work on this holiday!

Other workers, such as restaurant employees, transportation employees, and essential service employees like nurses, police, and firefighters, also must go to work on Labor Day.

Many fine examples of public art reflect our respect for working women and men.

A *Hammering Man* sculpture stands outside the Seattle Art Museum. The hammering arm "works," moving up and down, every day of the year except one: on Labor Day, it rests.

A sculpture of the *Hammering Man* outside the Seattle Art Museum

Other *Hammering Man* sculptures stand in cities around the world. The sculptures were created to honor all workers, everywhere.

These sculptures and many others remind us that all work is honorable and important.

The Garment Worker sculpture in New York, NY

A statue dedicated to railroad workers in Flagstaff, AZ

Not every worker belongs to a union. But every worker is important—and we celebrate all of them on Labor Day.

For kids, the most important job is school. Doing a good job in school is the best way to prepare for doing a good job as an adult. And it's the best way to contribute to our country's future success.

"The basic bargain of America is that
no matter who you are,
where you come from, or
what you look like,
if you work hard and
play by the rules,
you can make it."
—Secretary of Labor Thomas Edward Perez